CAMBRII

Ghost

Prepare to be frightened by these terrifying tales from around Cambridgeshire

By

Richard Holland

BRADWELL
BOOKS

Published by Bradwell Books
9 Orgreave Close Sheffield S13 9NP
Email: books@bradwellbooks.co.uk

British Library Cataloguing in Publication Data: a catalogue
record for this book is available from the British Library.

1st Edition

ISBN: 9781902674742

Print: Gomer Press, Llandysul, Ceredigion SA44 4JL

Design by: jenksdesign@yahoo.co.uk

Picture Credits: Joe McIntyre, Simon Middleton, ShutterStock
and Richard Holland

CONTENTS

The statue of Oliver Cromwell at St Neots. The Lord Protector of England's ghost has been encountered at several locations in Cambridgeshire.
Guy Erwood/Shutterstock

INTRODUCTION

Cambridgeshire is extraordinarily rich in history. Now incorporating old Huntingdonshire and the Soke of Peterborough, it is one of the counties which comprise East Anglia. For centuries Cambridgeshire was a marshy wilderness, a region of extensive fens surrounding low-lying islands, the only high point for miles around being the mysterious Gogmagog Hills with their ancient, enigmatic rock carvings.

The isolated nature of the Fens created small communities, whose self-sufficiency and isolation, as well as the extraordinary environment in which they lived, inspired a rich and unique folklore. The area was one of the last places in England to fend off the invading Normans. It was a difficult landscape to penetrate and an ideal one for guerilla warfare. The glorious cathedrals of Peterborough and Ely testify to the fact that in time the Normans made it their own.

Many of Cambridgeshire's reported ghosts are shades of its monastic past. Phantom monks, robed in the black habits of the Benedictine order, are legion. So, too, are 'Grey Ladies', most of which are probably apparitions of nuns. On the whole, these are peaceful haunters, their afterlives spent as quietly and unassumingly as their lives. Others are noisier and more dramatic. They include highwaymen, riotous squires, Civil War soldiers, knights on horseback and a black-clad man who drags a coffin down a flight of stairs. There are also animal ghosts, in particular the alarming Black Dogs – huge, hellish hounds that pad along dark lanes and tracks through the Fens. The animal ghost that haunted two locations in Cambridge remains one of the most enigmatic in English ghostlore, a weird furry thing with a beak which scampered about on two legs!

Cambridgeshire also has more than its fair share of 'celebrity' ghosts. These include two poets, the infamous 'Bloody Mary' and the warrior-politician Oliver Cromwell, who changed the course of English history and whose domineering spirit succeeds in still making its presence known in a number of places.

The extraordinary haunted heritage of Cambridgeshire is one of its less obvious attractions. Far more apparent to visitor and resident alike are its great natural beauty, including rare survivals of England's fenland, harbouring unique animal and plant life, and the beauty of its anciently inhabited villages, stately homes and, of course, those world-famous colleges.

It is a county well worth exploring, one which can surprise and delight at any turn. My thanks to my friends Joe McIntyre and Simon Middleton, Cambridge residents, who kindly took up my offer to carry out some spooky expeditions of their own, armed with their cameras. Their photographs of some of Cambridgeshire's most haunted locations are a real bonus for *Cambridgeshire Ghost Stories*.

Richard Holland

THE CAMBRIDGE COLLEGES

Cambridge is known worldwide for its famous university, one of the oldest and most prestigious in Britain. Its origin dates back to the 13th century when Oxford scholars, on the run from hostile townsfolk, ended up in Cambridge. The scholars organised themselves into groups in which those who successfully completed their studies taught newcomers. This system continued for many years and individual colleges were founded thanks to wealthy patronage. Most of Cambridge University's colleges are of medieval origin and boast magnificent Gothic buildings, including dormitories which have boarded celebrities in the arts and sciences from the Middle Ages through to the present day, and will continue to do so. Centuries of history combined with this hothouse atmosphere have apparently proved the ideal breeding ground for ghosts.

In the Fellows' Garden of **Christ's College** can be found one of Cambridge's more charming landmarks: an ancient mulberry tree which tradition states as having been planted by the poet John Milton on his graduation in 1633. Despite being nearly 400 years old, it still bears fruit. Tradition has it that on moonlit nights a ghost can be seen wandering round the tree. However, this is not Milton, but a Victorian academic, Christopher Round. Daniel Codd, in his excellent *Mysterious Cambridgeshire* (DB Publishing 2010), describes the apparition as that of 'a tall, stooped elderly-looking man … his hands clasped behind his back as though he is deep in sombre contemplation'.

It is said that, on his death bed, Round confessed to a murder that had gone undetected. He said that one night he happened to see one Philip Collier staggering round the grounds as if he was drunk. Round hated Collier: not only were they bitter academic rivals, they were also rivals in love, for the heart of a girl called Mary Clifford. As Round watched, Collier stumbled and fell into a private swimming pool in the Fellows' Garden. Rather disgusted by Collier's supposed drunkenness, he hurried over to help him, picking up a boat-hook with which to drag him out of the water. But then he realised this was an opportunity to get Collier out of the way and, almost without thinking, he brought the boat-hook crashing down on his hated rival's head. He walked away, leaving Collier to drown.

There was a tragic and unlooked for sequel to this act, however. Unbeknownst to the murderer, Collier had not been drunk that night. He had been experimenting with anaesthetics, a study then still in its infancy. Mary, the girl they both loved, suffered from a progressive illness and Collier had been seeking ways to ease her pain. With his death, of course, the experiments ceased and in time Mary, too, died – in dreadful and perhaps preventable agony. For forty years, the remorseful Round took to pacing about Milton's mulberry tree at night, unable to sleep, and is supposedly pacing still. According to veteran ghost-hunter Peter Underwood, heavy footsteps are heard clumping up the staircase to the first floor of the college. Possibly they too belong to Christopher Round.

*Christ's College, haunted by a remorseful old don who committed
an undiscovered murder.*
BasPhoto/Shutterstock

Two ghosts are said to haunt **Corpus Christi**. The best known is that of Dr Henry Butts, a former Master of the college and Chancellor of the university. It was his unlucky lot to see the university through an outbreak of plague in 1630. It was a miserable time for him, watching colleagues and students die and holding the fort with fewer and fewer people for company. In a letter to a colleague he described himself as 'a destitute and forsaken man, not a Scholler with me in College, not a Scholler seen by me without.' The experience seems to have brought on a permanent depression and he remained a broken man. On Easter Sunday 1632, he was found in his rooms in the Old Lodge in Old Court, hanging by his garters. It is said that, ever since his tragic death, Dr Butts's unhappy spirit has haunted his former rooms.

On one occasion the ghost was seen in broad daylight by an undergraduate working in rooms which happened to face those formerly occupied by Dr Butts. A creepy feeling came over the student and he looked up to see a man glaring at him across the court. With his long hair drooping down on either side of his face, the man was leaning out of a window but, despite his fierce expression, he remained totally still, almost like a photograph. Wondering who on earth – or elsewhere – he could be, the undergrad ran upstairs to get a better view of the stranger, only to find he had gone. He made his way back downstairs again, and hurried across the court, but found the door locked. He later learnt from the owner of the rooms that he had been out that afternoon.

Someone then remembered the story of Dr Butts's ghost and the student got hold of an acquaintance with some experience of spiritualism and asked him and four other friends to join him in a séance. The séance was held in his own rooms, rather than those alleged to be haunted, but when the students commanded Dr Butts's spirit to appear, it did so (although only two of the company saw it). First they saw a mist in the room, which steadily grew more solid until they could clearly make out a man in the midst of it, with a gash on the side of his neck. Having succeeded in calling up the spirit, they became frightened and foolishly tried to repel it with a crucifix. They were driven back from the ghost by an invisible force and the séance descended into chaos.

According to Rupert Matthews in his *Haunted Cambridge* (Pitkin 1994) this was not the last sighting of Dr Butts. He writes: 'His phantom continues to move around Old Court and has been blamed for mysterious thumps and bangs which occur from time to time.' Matthews says he has also been encountered 'in rooms on the staircase of the original sighting'.

There is one other ghost at Corpus Christi, and he haunts the College Kitchen. The story behind this haunting is that another former master of the college, a Dr Spencer, discovered his daughter had a boyfriend and went on the warpath. In order to escape his wrath, the terrified youth hid in a cupboard in the kitchen. Unfortunately, he became trapped and suffocated, with the result that he has joined Dr Butts as a ghostly inhabitant of the college.

The Old Court, Corpus Christi College, where the clumsy exorcism of the spirit of Dr Henry Butts led to terror for a number of undergraduates.
DavidYoung/Shutterstock

In the early 19th century the Master of **Trinity College** was Christopher Wordsworth, brother of William, the Lakeland poet. Dr Wordsworth became curious about a suite of rooms which, despite being comfortable and convenient, kept being abandoned by the students billeted there. When a young freshman turned up at his door at the start of the academic year with a letter of introduction and asked him to recommend suitable accommodation, Dr Wordsworth saw an opportunity to satisfy his curiosity. Shortly after recommending the mysteriously unpopular rooms, he approached the student and asked him how he was finding them. The young man promptly told him that 'the rooms were very comfortable but that he should be obliged to give them up'. He explained that 'he had been awakened every night by the apparition of a child, which wandered about the rooms moaning'.

Dr Wordsworth admitted that he had heard a rumour the rooms were haunted but that 'having a perfect reliance on his judgment and veracity … he was desirous of seeing whether he would confirm the story, having had no intimation of it beforehand'. The student's reply on discovering he had been used in this way by Dr Wordsworth is not recorded, nor has any explanation for the haunting by the child come to light.

In 1922 T C Lethbridge, who later became a noted paranormal investigator, was with a fellow student when the door to his friend's room in New Court opened and a man wearing a top hat strode in. The intruder placed his hands in a rather purposeful manner on a table in the middle of the room. It was late and Lethbridge had been on the point of leaving anyway, so, assuming the man was one of the college porters needing to speak to his friend, he made his goodbyes and left. The next day he learnt that the friend had seen no one enter the room; in fact he hadn't even seen the door open. Trying to recall the mysterious figure in more detail, Lethbridge realised it was only the presence of the top hat that had made him think the man was a porter; on reflection, the rest of his outfit suggested he was wearing hunting kit. The incident baffled Lethbridge to the end of his life.

Trinity College's chapel was also haunted for a while. During the 1950s the clerk and organist in the chapel were discomfited on several occasions to see joining the congregation a Fellow who had previously died. In life, this man had taken his religion

Several ghosts haunt Trinity College, the most famous of which is that of a child which 'wandered about ... moaning'.
Jan Michaelsen/Shutterstock

seriously and had never missed Sunday service; for a while his spirit apparently continued to attend even after his body had been laid in the ground. Finally, an 'unaccountable feeling of unease' experienced by many on the stairs in Kings' Hostel is believed to date from the time when a Fellow, returning from a dinner party where he had imbibed 'not wisely but too well', tripped, fell backwards and broke his neck.

On June 4, 1930, a **King's College** medical student named Potts went mad and murdered two men in his tutor's rooms. One was a policeman, PC Willis, the other his tutor, Alexander

Wollaston. He was being questioned over the illegal possession of a firearm, when he suddenly produced the weapon. After shooting Willis and Wollaston, he turned the gun on himself and ended his own life. From time to time, it is said, the sounds of gunshots can still be heard emanating from this room, an echo of the tragedy.

In 1997 it was reported in the national press that the Dean of **Peterhouse College** was considering holding an exorcism after two colleagues told him they had seen the ghost of a man dressed after the style of the 18th century floating through a room which connects to the Fellows' dining room. One of the witnesses was the Senior Bursar, who told the press: 'It was wearing a wide collar, like a pilgrim, and seemed to be holding a large hat. I moved closer to get a better look. After a few seconds it quietly disappeared.'

In the 1960s an exorcism had been carried out in an attempt to banish the restless spirit of a former Bursar of Peterhouse, Francis Dawes, who had committed suicide in the college in 1789. It seemed reasonable to suppose that this was the same ghost, making a comeback after thirty years. The fact that it appeared to a fellow Bursar may not have been coincidence.

After a portrait of King Charles I was hung in Hall Court in **Sidney Sussex College**, weird things began to happen. There were reports of 'spooky noises' and sightings of an ill-defined spectre stalking about. The spirit of Oliver Cromwell was immediately suspected, for Sidney Sussex had been the college of the future Lord Protector and a painting of the king he had had beheaded was bound to upset him. Cromwell's own

*An exorcism has been carried out at Peterhouse College in order to
lay to rest the wandering spirit of a former Bursar.*
Adrian Zenz/Shutterstock

decapitated head (his corpse had been dug up and the head removed after the Restoration of Charles II) was interred here in a secret ceremony in 1960 after being in private hands for centuries. Ever since the burial there have been rumours that the ghost of Cromwell's disembodied bonce has been seen floating about the grounds.

No less strange is the second ghost of Sidney Sussex College. In 1967 an undergraduate reported seeing a disembodied purple eye glaring at him in his darkened room (one source describes it as 'bright blue'). He wasn't taken very seriously but this weird apparition seems to have a history: it was also seen in the 1840s. Who – or what – it formerly belonged to remains a mystery, which is possibly just as well.

Two very unusual spooks are said to haunt the precincts of Sidney Sussex College.
Amra Pasic/Shutterstock

A former Master of **St John's College**, James Wood (1760–1839), is said to haunt a staircase in the Second Court. He doesn't appear as the bearded old don you might expect, however, but as a threadbare young student. In his student days at the college, he lived in a garret here and, being very poor and unable to pay for candles or coal, he would sit on the stairs, his feet wrapped in straw to keep them warm, and by the dim illumination of a rush light, attempt to study his books. He may well have been full of misery and doubt during these difficult times and that is why his wan and shivering ghost is still to be seen here.

Much the weirdest ghost of Cambridge University – stranger even than floating heads and disembodied eyes – is the thing that infested one of the old buildings forming part of St John's, a black-and-white Tudor-period house now called Merton College. In her book on *Cambridgeshire Customs and Folklore* (Routledge & Kegan Paul 1969), Enid Porter relates an account of a spook which took the form of 'a furry animal that walked on its hind legs and had flipper-like front paws and a long beak'. Porter was informed of the existence of this phantom penguin-thing by a former Fellow of the University, who told her it would suddenly appear, now here, now there, in Merton College and could never be caught. It has been suggested it was the apparition of a 17th-century doctor wearing the peculiar costume adopted when treating plague victims: the outfit included a long 'beak' stuffed with aromatic herbs which they believed would protect them from the disease. The Merton College spook was much, much smaller than a man, however. The spook had previously manifested in Abbey House in Barnwell, Cambridge (see the next chapter), when the children of the house would be startled by its sudden appearance under their beds. They soon grew used to it, though, and enjoyed chasing it as it rapidly waddled through the house. This was in the early 1900s. By the 1920s it had, for some reason, transferred its meaningless activity to Merton College. In 1924, Porter was told, it was successfully exorcised.

The impressive entrance to St John's College. Two ghosts haunt St John's. One of them is arguably Cambridgeshire's weirdest spook.
Pres Panayotov/Shutterstock

Finally, **Jesus College** is the setting for one of the most famous ghost stories attached to Cambridge University. The story refers to the Everlasting Club, a Hellfire-type affair started by young bloods who were students at Jesus College in the 1720s. Every November they would hold their annual dinner, a particularly riotous and debauched occasion, in a room in the college. One year the members had a shock which made many of them reconsider their disreputable lives. The previous year one of their number, more drunk than usual, had died when he was run down by a horse and carriage. Imagine their horror when this deceased member appeared among them at their dinner and sat down in his usual place! The ghost glared meaningfully round at them, then vanished. From that time on, the Everlasting Club was cursed: one by one, the members each died a violent death, and then returned as ghosts to terrify those remaining.

It's a grim and ghastly story – and an example of a work of fiction having such an impact that it becomes folklore and is accepted as truth. The yarn was written by Sir Arthur Gray, who published it along with other stories about Cambridge life in a slim volume in 1919 when he was Master of Jesus College. Its constant retelling to undergraduates, backed up by the showing of a bricked-up window, supposedly the room used by the Everlasting Club and now sealed off for ever, has woven it into the fabric of Jesus College life. Although few probably believe the story, fewer still are aware that it is a piece of published fiction, rather than an old tradition.

A persistent tale is told about Jesus College featuring a disreputable club with an increasing number of ghostly members.
Raedwald/Shutterstock

MORE FROM CAMBRIDGE

Barnwell is now a suburb to the south of Cambridge. An Augustinian Priory was built here in 1112, having originally been founded at Castle End in Cambridge itself. It suffered along with most other ecclesiastical establishments in Henry VIII's Dissolution of the Monasteries and by the 17th century there was little of it left, most of its fabric having been carted away for use in later buildings. In 1659 a comfortable house was built on the site, incorporating what little was left of the medieval Priory. Today the house is known as the Abbey House.

For many years the Abbey House was haunted by a 'Grey Lady', believed to be a nun. She would be seen, dressed in grey robes, sweeping through the panelled walls as if they did not exist. The ghost was particularly active in the early years of the 20th century. The families of two or three university dons would share the commodious house at any one time, so there were plenty of witnesses around to catch a glimpse of her. The children of the house had no choice but to see her, for she made a particular habit of appearing by their bedsides after dark. Although they 'did not like her very much', the youngsters soon got used to the Grey Lady's nocturnal visits.

Tradition states that the ghost is that of a nun who belonged to a Benedictine nunnery on the site of Jesus College. Contrary to their vows, she and the canon at the Barnwell Priory had become lovers. They would meet using a subterranean tunnel that connected the convent with the old Priory (in the vaulted cellars below Abbey House, one archway is bricked up and this is thought to be where the tunnel originally opened). In stories such as this the relationships never end well and although this particular legend is incomplete, we might fairly speculate that the lovers were caught and both put to death. The usual punishment for a nun caught breaking her vow of chastity was to wall her up alive: did this fate befall the Grey Lady of Abbey House? Perhaps she's behind that brick wall in the cellar!

According to ghost-hunter Peter Underwood, 'a deathly white, disembodied woman's head' was seen floating about Abbey House in the 1920s and this too may have been a manifestation of the nun's ghost.

In complete contrast to a quiet nun, the other ghost of Abbey House is that of a rollicking old squire of the 18th century. In life he was Squire Jacob Butler, who stood six-and-a-half feet tall and was muscular with it. Squire Butler lived a rambunctious life, drinking and playing hard and with a fondness for practical jokes. His noisy spirit still clumps and thumps about the house.

Abbey House was also the original haunt of the strange animal-like phantom which later transferred its activities to St John's College (see above). Although it was reported that the entity had been successfully exorcised in the 1920s, claims have been made of the oddity having been seen on Newmarket Road, not far from the Abbey House, in more recent times.

Trumpington Street in the town centre is one of Cambridge's most attractive thoroughfares, overlooked by many beautiful old buildings. An odd and oft-repeated story is that during the reign of Victoria, a woman was being shown round a house in Trumpington Street with a view to buying it (another source describes the visitor as 'a man from London'). On her (or his) tour she was particularly struck by a painting in the drawing room, a full-length portrait of a woman in a green gown dating, judging by the fashion, from the previous century. As the visitor was being shown out, the owner lightly mentioned the tradition that the house was haunted by a woman in green. 'The woman in the portrait?' asked the potential buyer. The owner was puzzled. What picture did she mean? When they returned to the drawing room, the visitor was startled to discover that the painting of the woman in green was nowhere to be seen, nor was there a space on the wall to hang it.

The other phantom female haunting Trumpington Street is less enigmatic. She is the ghost of the first wife of a Master of Peterhouse College. An old hostelry, The Little Rose, was a favourite hangout of students at Peterhouse and several lodged there. This kind-hearted lady served as a surrogate mother for these young undergraduates and spent many happy times in the inn, which she now haunts. The Little Rose recently became the Loch Fyne Restaurant, but a centuries-old emblem of a rose in plaster on the frontage is still clearly visible as a reminder of its original name.

The emblem of a rose on the frontage of this Trumpington Street restaurant reveals that for centuries it was an inn called The Little Rose. It is haunted by the wife of a former Master of Peterhouse College.
© Joe McIntyre / Simon Middleton

Peterhouse College features in another spooky legend. Just off Trumpington Street is the **Church of St Mary the Less**. The church's cemetery is entered through a stone gate. Squatting malevolently on top of this gate was a dark, paranormal presence which some believed to be the angry spirit of William Dowling, a strict Puritan who was obsessed with ripping Roman Catholic imagery from churches after the Civil War, including St Mary the Less. The dark shape would glower at the Peterhouse dormitories across the way and a grim rumour started that students whose windows overlooked the cemetery were prone to taking their own lives. This baleful influence was removed for good after college authorities arranged an exorcism here in the 1960s.

Running alongside the church is the charming **Little St Mary's Lane**, whose appearance has barely changed in two hundred years. Its ghost is equally charming and a cheerful contrast to the malignant spirit of the cemetery gate. A small girl in a frilly dress of the Victorian period, bedecked with ribbons, she scampers smiling down the street. It is unknown who she was in life, nor why she haunts the lane.

We have heard much of ghostly dons in the previous chapter. Another has been seen strolling down **Parker Street** and **St Andrew's Street** in a grey suit. He was a tutor at Christ's College who was found drowned in a popular bathing pool in the River Cam. Although this was officially considered an accident, rumour had it he was murdered by a rival for a girl's affections.

Little St Mary's Lane has barely changed its appearance for centuries.
The apparition of a little girl in Victorian costume must feel right at home here.
© *Joe McIntyre / Simon Middleton*

Another intellectual ghost is that of John Pink, the first librarian of the **Central Library**, who took up his post in 1853. Soon after his death, Pink's apparition was seen in the library, pottering about the books as if to make sure they were being correctly shelved in his absence. His most popular haunt was the iron gallery, a feature of the original Victorian construction. From the library to The Haunted Bookshop. Situated in **St Edward's Passage**, connecting King's Parade and Peas Hill, this second-hand bookshop has not one but two ghosts on its premises. The shade of a hefty man dressed in dark clothes of the Victorian age hangs about in the cellar while the apparition of a blonde-haired woman in a pale dress drifts around the upper rooms. The street-level, public salesrooms are never visited by the ghosts, which means neither knows anything about the other, which seems a bit of a shame, especially if they are both book-lovers.

There are several more spectral women in Cambridge. In **Montague Road**, a young boy saw on several occasions a pretty young woman swinging idly back and forth in a hammock slung between two trees in his back garden. The apparition was later identified as that of a girl who had died of a wasting disease in the house years previously. During her last summer on earth she often spent her days in the hammock soaking up the sun and enjoying the fresh air. A woman in black haunted a house in **Sidney Park** for a number of years. Then one day human bones were found in the garden and given a Christian burial. After that the haunting ceased (Sidney Park has itself disappeared under modern retail development). South of Cambridge, on Hills Road, **Addenbrooke's Hospital** is haunted by a nurse but she only appears when morphia is

The Haunted Bookshop in St Edward's Passage is so named because
of the two ghosts on its premises.
© *Joe McIntyre / Simon Middleton*

administered to a patient. It is thought she may have been guilty of accidentally giving too high a dose to a patient during her time at the hospital and, full of remorse, returns to make sure the error doesn't occur again.

We must be grateful that the final female phantom in this list now no longer haunts the county, for although she was described as 'a gentlewoman' she was far from gentle; in fact she was a killer! For some reason that remains unexplained this frightening entity latched on to a youth from Ely named Franklin who was working as an apprentice in Cambridge. She would appear before Franklin on numerous occasions and initially they were on as friendly terms as a young man and a ghostly woman can be. According to Richard Baxter, in his *The Certainty of the World of Spirits* (1692), 'she and he were very free and had long been wont to disport together, even while company was in the room'. The spirit was angry Franklin had left Ely and kept trying to persuade him to return there. They had a row, and the ghost struck him a severe blow on his forehead. The next morning it was found that Franklin was very ill. The man to whom he was apprenticed was so worried about him that he rode over to Ely to alert the boy's father.

Later on that day, Franklin and the lady of the house were warming themselves by the fire when he suddenly cried out: 'O, mistress look! There's the gentlewoman!' She peered about but was unable to see the ghost. But then she heard a horrible thud and she turned back to see that Franklin's head was drooping: his neck had been broken. At about the same time her husband and the youth's father were sitting down together in Ely discussing what might be done about Franklin when the woman's ghost appeared in the room. She glared at them both, her face a mask of fury, then vanished. Some time later, when poor Franklin's body was viewed, there was visible on his forehead a red mark just where the fatal phantom had struck him the previous day.

PETERBOROUGH

The Soke of Peterborough is an ancient demarcation dating from before the Norman Conquest. The word 'soke' – coincidentally so suggestive of the damp, marshy ground in which Peterborough is situated – refers to the right to free jurisdiction as enjoyed by the Anglo-Saxon bigwigs. The right was continued after the Conquest by the Abbots of Peterborough and the parish is still considered as belonging to Northamptonshire, even though the Soke has now been incorporated into Cambridgeshire.

That such a historic city should have numerous ghosts is perhaps no surprise, and some of them are very old indeed. One of the few surviving copies of the *Anglo-Saxon Chronicle*, originally compiled in the 9th century, was extended and updated at Peterborough Abbey. Under the date 1127, the monk continuing the manuscript writes of the general dislike of the appointment at Peterborough of a Norman abbot, Henry of Poitou. According to him, Henry 'did nothing good there and left nothing good there'. Worse still, his arrival in Peterborough saw the advent of a terrifying haunting beyond the city's bounds: the Wild Hunt. The Wild Hunt took the form of hunters, described as 'big and loathsome', hunting with equally 'loathsome' hounds and riding black horses and, more devilish still, black goats. The sound of their hunting horns kept the monks and the townspeople awake and trembling at night.

This is the earliest record of the Wild Hunt in England. The phenomenon was once believed in throughout Europe. Some thought they were the spirits of aristocrats hunting through the forests and linked them to heroic personalities like Wild Edric (in Shropshire) and King Herla (in Monmouthshire/ Herefordshire). Others thought they were fairies. Most alarming was the belief that they were demons hunting wicked souls and harrying them to hell. In this guise the Wild Hunt appears in many forms, as the Yeth Hounds of Devon and the Gabriel Ratchets of northern England. The Peterborough chronicler does not expound on the 'loathsome' hunters' nature or origin; for him they were simply a hellish presence reflecting a period of discord.

There has been a church on the site of **Peterborough Cathedral** since Anglo-Saxon times. This was enlarged and made an abbey in the 10th century, which in turn was enlarged to become a cathedral after the Norman Conquest. Today it is considered one of the best-preserved 12th-century buildings in Britain. The magnificent West Front has been voted one of the top ten best views in England – but how many of the thousands who photograph it every year are aware that it is haunted?

The ghost is said to be one of the 12th-century builders, a dedicated stonemason who on one fatal occasion worked late into the night, perched high up on rickety scaffolding. Finally growing too tired to work, he blew out his candle and then realised he was now deprived of sufficient light to find his way down. He scrabbled for his flint to relight the candle, but, failing

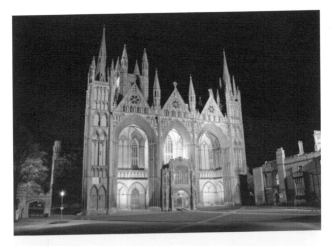

*Peterborough's majestic cathedral is haunted by a medieval stonemason
and a number of anonymous monks.*
Liubov Terletska/Shutterstock

to find it, gingerly tried to find his way down. Alas, he slipped and fell to his death. The flickering light sometimes seen behind the windows high up on the West Front is said to be a phantasm of the candle the stonemason so desperately wished for. The mason himself has also been seen, forlornly chiselling away at the window frame he was prevented from finishing.

In common with many ecclesiastical buildings, Peterborough Cathedral is also haunted by numerous anonymous phantom monks. Stuart Orme, author of *Haunted Peterborough* (History Press 2012) has compiled a fairly extensive inventory of them. Dressed in the black hoods and gowns of the Benedictine order, they have been seen in the cloisters, on an external passage leading to the cloisters, in the graveyard to the north of the cathedral and elsewhere in the precincts. The most interesting is that which has been seen making his way up the nave. Unlike the other monks, his hood is thrown back and his face, very young and scared, can be clearly seen. Near the altar, he turns as if aware that a pursuer has caught up with him. He then flees further up the nave and vanishes under the great tower.

Another phantom monk has been seen in the eastern suburbs of Peterborough. One witness told the press: 'Last Friday I was in the lane proceeding from **Dogsthorpe** to **Garton End**. It would be about ten minutes to ten, and suddenly, right in front of me, at about 20 to 30 yards away, appeared a black hooded figure of about five feet in height. The hood came right down to the ground, and the figure seemed to be gliding along two or three feet from the footpath. I at once bolted forward, and as I did so the figure glided rapidly away, and seemed to melt through the hedge…'

Another spooky figure in black became a terror to the neighbourhood of **Woodston**. So alarming did the locals find her that they put up signs which read 'Beware the ghost of the Lady in Black'. The 'Lady in Black' would most often be seen in the graveyard of St Augustine's Church and the lane which runs alongside it. She was believed to be a widow from Belsize Avenue who, on her death bed, insisted she would come back from the grave to look after her orphaned children. This hardly sounds like a very menacing ghost but Woodston residents were terrified of her. A gang of young men armed themselves with stakes and went out in the dark, determined 'to lay her ghost

Phantom monks in black habits are among the most commonly reported
apparitions in Cambridgeshire, particularly in Peterborough and Ely.
mogen creative/Shutterstock

once and for all'. They returned hours later, minus their stakes and in a state of communal nervous collapse. It is possible they had gone to the churchyard with the intention of digging up the lady's grave and staking her body to the earth to prevent her from 'walking' but it's unclear. All this took place in 1908. The children were taken to live elsewhere and the 'Lady in Black' was no longer seen in Woodston.

According to Stuart Orme, there are numerous ghosts in the **City Centre**, including a former security guard who still patrols the Town Hall; a couple dressed in the fashions of the 1930s, in Priestgate; a Georgian man and a Victorian woman, in Cowgate; and a raggedy child of an indeterminate period who has been seen in the glittering interior of the Queensgate shopping centre.

In their book, *Shadows In The Steam* (History Press 2009), Peterborough-based authors David Brandon and Alan Brooke tell of a mysterious passenger who entered a carriage at **Peterborough Railway Station** only to vanish many miles further up the line. The elderly woman was dressed in the height of Victorian fashion, all in black, and was carrying a basket. She smiled pleasantly at the existing occupants of the carriage, a newly married husband and wife, then settled into her seat, the young couple eyeing her with some bemusement. At Grantchester there was a slight delay and the husband popped out for refreshments. Since there were only three people sharing the carriage, it occurred to him that perhaps he should buy a cup of tea for the oddly dressed lady, too. She accepted with a smile but without actually saying anything. The journey north continued. The antiquated old lady closed her eyes and appeared to doze but as the train entered Durham Station, she made moves to get out. The young man politely took her basket as she clambered out and then handed it to her. For the first time, she spoke: 'I wish you many happy years,' she said. And with that, she vanished!

Hauntings also occur in the surrounding rail network. The sounds of the gates opening and closing have been heard at **Conington Crossing** and the apparition of an old-fashioned Chrysler car is sometimes seen here: eerie echoes of a fatal accident in which a train smashed into a car crossing the line in 1948. The scenic Nene Valley Railway also has its ghosts. A white cat haunts the **Yarwell Tunnel**. She was the pet of a former stationmaster at Wansford. She wandered into the tunnel and her owner, fearing for her safety, followed her – but it was he who was killed by an oncoming train, not the cat, so the haunting is an unusual one. It is possible that he haunts **Wansford Station** itself, however, for here the opening and closing of doors by unseen hands has been observed and heavy stamping footsteps heard in empty rooms.

The most haunted building in Peterborough appears to be its **museum**. There are a number of haunted museums in the UK, perhaps because they contain so many remnants of past times and past lives. Many are also housed in old and historic buildings, including Peterborough's, a Georgian mansion in Priestgate created out of a 16th-century property. Before it was a museum, it was the Infirmary (and hospitals are places where paranormal activity is reported far more often than museums). Its best-known ghost is believed to date from that time and is said to be of 'the lonely ANZAC', an Australian soldier who died in the Infirmary in 1916. The plight of this young soldier,

Ghostly phenomena have been reported from Wansford Station on the scenic Nene Valley Railway.
i4lcocl2/Shutterstock

who died so far from home, touched the people of Peterborough and subscriptions paid for a granite monument on his grave and a plaque in the military chapel of the cathedral. He began to haunt the hospital soon after his death and was positively identified by nurses working there. Today he appears as a shadowy figure dressed in grey, usually seen on the main staircase.

The swishing of a lady's full-length dress has been heard on this staircase and also female voices. On one occasion a shrill voice was heard to call out: 'Lady Charlotte!' This possibly refers to Charlotte Cooke, who was a member of the family which built the grand Georgian house. In *Haunted Peterborough*, Stuart Orme

Peterborough Museum is one of the most haunted buildings in Cambridgeshire. Many of its ghosts appear to date from the time when it was used as an infirmary.
© *Tim Galley*

writes: 'On a number of occasions, when locking up the museum after an evening tour around the museum, I have been so convinced I have heard two women muttering together on the stairs that I thought I must have locked someone in the building by mistake.'

Other ghosts encountered in the museum include a kindly-looking doctor; a little girl wandering among the fossil exhibits; a woman in white and, by contrast, a 'dark man' on the top floor; and possibly the spirit of a Roman soldier, watching over a sword of the period which is now on display. In addition, a range of other spooky phenomena have been reported, such as strange noises, anomalous smells (including that of the kind of disinfectant dating used when the building was a hospital), and most worryingly, pushing and shoving from invisible entities. It's amazing anyone has time to enjoy the exhibits!

ELY

Cambridgeshire's other cathedral city is Ely, the Isle of Eels, which is no less historic than Peterborough and boasts an equally beautiful cathedral church. Nicknamed 'the ship of the Fens' thanks to its distinctive tall-masted shape, the cathedral has a similar history to that of Peterborough. A church was founded here by an Anglo-Saxon princess, St Aethelthryth, or Etheldreda, in the 7th century. This was later expanded to become a Benedictine monastery, which was made a cathedral in 1109. After the Norman Conquest, the cathedral and its associated monastery were greatly enlarged over a number of years. Today Ely is still possessed of one of the most extensive collections of surviving medieval monastic buildings in Britain. Huddled within the cathedral close, they are collectively known as 'the College'.

Cathedral and College together offer the most haunted location in Ely, perhaps in all of Cambridgeshire. St Etheldreda herself is claimed as one of the ghosts. The saint's relics were kept at Ely, survived an attack by the Vikings, and were moved about from church to cathedral to cathedral chapel. During Henry VIII's Dissolution of the Monasteries most of them were destroyed but her left hand was smuggled into the possession of successive Roman Catholic families in Ely. For a time it was kept at the **presbytery** in Ely, where its presence immediately ended the activity of a harmless but mischievous poltergeist. It now rests in a reliquary in St Etheldreda's Church in Holborn, London (whether this means the poltergeist has returned to the presbytery, I cannot say). The hand, or rather a ghostly version of it, is said to have made a reappearance in 1995, when boarders at the **Priory House** – part of King's Ely independent school, one of the oldest schools in the country – said they saw it on the back staircase. The boys described it as a disembodied hand, gliding up the banister and glowing with a rich blue light. Oddly enough, the actual relic was also a bluish-white until recent years, since when it has turned brown.

In common with Peterborough, the vast majority of the ghostly apparitions reported from Ely are those of black-habited Benedictine monks, and not surprisingly most of these have been seen in the cathedral or the College. We have two local ladies, Margaret Haynes and Vivienne Doughty, to thank for compiling these sightings and they can be found in their book *Haunted Ely* (Blue Hand Press 2003). In the **cathedral**, a phantom monk has been observed in the north triforium and another sitting in the 14th-century choir stalls, often during Evensong and sometimes with unsuspecting members of the congregation sitting near him. Two more have been known to take a stroll together in broad daylight on the grass between the cathedral gate and the 'Christopher Wren' door into the north transept.

A monk with no face within his cowl haunts the **Deanery**. He was an irregular and always unwelcome visitor to an attic bedroom used by novelist Elizabeth Goudge when she was a young girl. 'He was not a pleasant person,' Goudge recalled. Her father, then in charge of the Theological School, agreed to let her change her room but the ghost followed her there. According to Goudge, the monk was seen by many subsequent residents of the house. This was partly confirmed in 1992 when the wife of the precentor told the *Ely Cathedral News* about the mysterious

Numerous ghosts have been seen in and around Ely's glorious medieval cathedral.
martin garnham/Shutterstock

footsteps that had a habit of invading the room, much to her discomfort. She would always dive under the bed covers whenever the steps approached, however, so never saw what was making them.

More anonymous cowled figures have been encountered in the **Goldsmith's Tower**; on a path which passes the **Oyster Lane** entrance to the Deanery; and on a path which leads to the **Almonry Gate**. The monk haunting **Powcher's Hall** is a rather more cheerful specimen: he peers out of a little window, a big grin on his face.

Another venerable haunted building highlighted by Haynes and Doughty is a medieval hall house in **Silver Street**, long since converted to several smaller cottages. Most of them are named after the ancient wall paintings uncovered in the 1980s: Vine Cottage, Dove Cottage etc. A number of the cottages are haunted by a family whose costume suggests they lived in the hall house centuries ago. They are unaware of the more recent dividing walls and roam the separate dwellings at will. The 'father' is described as 'thirtyish, blond, about five foot nine' and wearing 'a white shirt with military trousers' and sometimes a leather jerkin and sacking trousers. His wife is shorter and has long, dark hair. There are three children: a boy of about ten, a girl of about four and an infant. They have been seen in the garden as well as the house. In addition, Vine Cottage is haunted by a man from an even earlier period, possibly from the time when the house was first built. Dressed all in black, he carries a silver cup round his neck, which implies he may have been a wine merchant.

Oliver Cromwell's House in the centre of Ely was the family home of the Cromwells for ten years before Oliver became England's first and only Lord Protector. Unlike the Silver Street cottages, it is open to the public and has become a museum, recreating a 17th-century home as the Cromwells might have known it. Oliver Cromwell himself is believed to haunt the house, as a 'brooding male presence' in one of the bedrooms. His may be the disembodied footfalls that are heard to pace about the upper floor. More commonly encountered is the apparition of a woman in a long blue dress with keys jingling at her waist. She may be one of the largely female household of the time of Cromwell's residency here, his wife or mother perhaps.

Incidentally, the Lord Protector's ghost has been seen elsewhere in Cambridgeshire. Between 1631 and 1636 he lived in **St Ives**, a fact commemorated by a statue in the market square. Opposite is the Golden Lion, a handsome old inn where Cromwell is said to have held meetings during the Civil War. The Golden Lion's 'Oliver Cromwell Room' is said to be haunted by him (and there are further reports of a ghostly Cavalier, Roundhead and a woman in a green dress, as well as poltergeist activity, haunting the hotel). Cromwell has also been stomping round the lanes near **Wisbech** and, over the border into Northamptonshire, at the site of the Battle of Naseby. His disembodied head, as we have seen, is said to haunt one of the colleges of Cambridge University.

Oliver Cromwell's House in Ely is haunted by a woman with keys attached to her waist, possibly Cromwell's mother. Cromwell himself may also haunt the house.
Guy Erwood/Shutterstock

TWO GRAND HOUSES

At the time of writing, one of the handsomest houses in Cambridgeshire, **Sawston Hall**, had recently been sold (for a rumoured £6 million) and it is uncertain whether it will be open to the public, used as a hotel or remain a private home. On an anciently inhabited site, the current house dates largely from the latter half of the 16th century. This is because the original hall suffered a disastrous fire in 1553. After the death of the sickly boy king Edward VI in that year, England was thrown into chaos, with different factions vying for the throne. For reasons of his own, John Dudley, the Duke of Northumberland, was determined to see it occupied by Lady Jane Grey, the king's cousin, rather than either of his sisters, Mary or Elizabeth Tudor. Although Edward had died, Dudley sent messages to Mary and Elizabeth that he was near death and that they should both come quickly to London to be at his bedside. It was a trap, of course. The older sister and true heir, Mary, took the bait (the shrewder Elizabeth claimed she was too ill to travel).

En route to London, Mary got wind of the plot and headed east in the hope of reaching safety. She decided to stay the night with a devout Roman Catholic family, the Huddlestons, at Sawston Hall. The Duke of Northumberland's son, Robert Dudley, had been dispatched with a company of armed men to apprehend Mary and somehow he learnt of her whereabouts. He and his soldiers besieged Sawston Hall. Perhaps the years practising their faith during the suppression of Catholicism under Henry VIII and his son had given the Huddlestons a sixth sense about unexpected and unwelcome visits but, at any rate, they had their wits about them, and smuggled Mary out of the house disguised as a kitchen maid. Infuriated at being unable to locate Mary,

Dudley's men torched the house in the hope it would drive her out. As she hurried away, the future queen turned back and saw the flames illuminating the night sky. 'Let it blaze,' she allegedly said. 'I would build Huddleston a better.'

Later a grateful Mary did indeed provide funds for Sawston Hall to be rebuilt. After the execution of Lady Jane Grey, she briefly reigned as Queen of England, restored Catholicism and persecuted Protestants with such brutality that she has earned herself the sobriquet of 'Bloody Mary'. She was executed in her turn and the far cannier Elizabeth became in her stead one of Britain's most popular monarchs. The apparition of a haughty woman in grey seen in various parts of Sawston Hall has been identified as Mary Tudor. One of its favourite haunts is the Tapestry Room, where Mary slept on that fateful night and where the four-poster bed she slept in is still to be seen. She has also been seen in the grounds.

One night the Panelled Room was disturbed by tramping footsteps every hour, like clockwork – possibly the ghost of a night-watchman. Other strange noises have been heard here. One afternoon a former owner heard what was described as 'a peal of female laughter' coming from an empty room. More frequently ghostly music of a past age has delighted the ear, trills on what has been identified as a spinet. In 1971 a ghost story, of a sort, was being filmed at Sawston Hall. This was *The Nightcomers*, directed by Michael Winner and starring Marlon Brando. It is a prequel to Henry James's classic tale, *The Turn of the Screw*, in which the spirits of dead servants apparently come back from beyond the grave to terrorise a governess. Two security guards employed to patrol the house – and film set – at

Mary Tudor, later Queen Mary I of England, escaped with her life from Sawston Hall but her austere presence still haunts the house, along with other ghosts.

night heard a different sort of music, that of a Mass, emanating from the chapel. When they went to investigate, they found it in silent darkness.

Another splendid Tudor mansion with a haunted reputation is **Madingley Hall**. It is somewhat larger than Sawston Hall and built mainly of old brick rather than Sawston's mellow stone. Close to the city, Madingley is owned by Cambridge University and is made available for events such as weddings and conferences. It too has links to royalty, as Edward VII slept in the King's Room while he was Prince of Wales. Local legend has it that another king, Charles I, hid here during his interminable tour round England after the tide of the Civil War turned against him.

The house was built in 1543 by Sir John Hynde. His wife, Ursula, is the traditional ghost of Madingley. She is said to have been furious with her son, Sir Francis, who took advantage of Henry VIII's Dissolution of the Monasteries to greatly extend the house and estate, even so far as ripping down the Church of St Etheldreda in Histon so he could make use of its stone and timber. The devout Ursula, who considered the family quite wealthy enough without this sacrilege, was thoroughly ashamed of this behaviour and her unhappy spirit has been seen on Christmas Eve, walking between the hall and the site of the church, wringing her hands in sorrow. She also haunts a room in one of the turrets, apparently choosing this chamber because it contains beams robbed from the church.

The ghost of Ursula Hyde is recalled in a poem by Rupert Brooke (see Grantchester in the next chapter). He wrote:

'And things go on you'd ne'er believe
At Madingley – on Christmas Eve.'

Two more women haunt Madingley Hall. One, known as 'Old Lady Cotton', has the habit of striding up the drive in a black dress. There are no details as to her origin or reason for haunting the hall. The other, by contrast, is dressed in white, for she was a young bride, a daughter of the house in the 17th century, who died of a broken heart when her intended lost his life a few days before her wedding. She has been seen sweeping across the courtyard. On one memorable occasion, when the house was being used by the military during the Second World War, a sentry challenged the spectral bride and then shot at her when she failed to respond.

Finally, there is the strange experience of a visitor to Madingley Hall in 1963. Joan Forman explains what happens in her book *Haunted East Anglia* (Jarrold 1974): 'A Cambridge woman who was accustomed to walking her dogs in the grounds of Madingley Hall called there one day when the grounds were closed to the public. As she approached the Hall she heard unmistakable sounds of human voices, and noticed particularly that of a woman – a deep laughing voice. She decided that she had intruded on a garden party, but a little later she had reason to revise that conclusion. At the top of the garden, near the house, she saw a young man sprawling over a stone balustrade. Whether he appeared to be dead or not is uncertain. She apparently thought his face resembled a death's head and to be contorted by hate as he looked at her. She noticed that he was wearing a ruff and that his hair was cut jaggedly across his forehead. Both the costume detail and the hairstyle suggest the 16th century, when the ruff was at its height of popularity and male hairstyles, though trimmed to show a high forehead, were yet combed forward unevenly at the front.'

The dog walker appeared to have had a sudden glimpse of some Elizabethan tragedy long since forgotten.

'Things go on you'd ne'er believe' at Madingley Hall.
© *Joe McIntyre / Simon Middleton*

FOUR MORE HAUNTED HOUSES

All the following are private homes and are not open to the public. In the village of **Barnack**, in old Huntingdonshire, can be found Kingsley House. This handsome medieval home was for many years the rectory. In the early 19th century the Rector of Barnack was the father of Charles Kingsley, author of *Westward Ho!* (1855) and *The Water Babies* (1863). The rectory was haunted by the ghost of a previous rector, who had defrauded his relatives and so could not rest easy in his grave. He was nicknamed 'Button Cap'. In a recollection of his childhood, Charles Kinglsey wrote:

'Button Cap … lived in the great north room at Barnack. I knew him well. He used to walk across the room in flopping slippers, and turn over the leaves of books to find the missing deed, whereof he had defrauded the orphan and the widow. He was an old Rector of Barnack. Everybody heard him who chose. Nobody ever saw him; but in spite of that, he wore a flowered dressing-gown, and a cap with a button on it.

'I never heard of any skeleton being found; and Button Cap's history had nothing to do with murder, only with avarice and cheating. Sometimes he turned cross and turned Poltergeist, as the Germans say, rolling the barrels in the cellar about with surprising noise, which was undignified. So he was always ashamed of himself, and put them all back in their places before morning.'

As a child Kingsley suffered an attack of 'brain fever' (whatever that is) and for some inexplicable reason was moved into the supposedly haunted room to recover. Jennifer Westwood and Jacqueline Simpson, writing about the ghost in their monumental book *The Lore Of The Land* (Penguin 2005), describe Kingsley as 'a nervous and highly sensitive boy', adding: 'For years afterwards, his imagination was haunted by the memory of the weird sights and sounds he experienced.'

Nevertheless, as a cynical grown-up, Kingsley felt able to write: 'I suppose he is gone now. Ghosts hate a certificated National Schoolmaster, and (being a vain and peevish generation) as soon as people give up believing in them, go away in a huff – or perhaps someone had been laying phosphoric paste about, and he ate thereof and ran down to the pond, and drank till he burst. He was rats!'

Kingsley House, formerly Barnack Rectory, was haunted by a character known as 'Button Cap'.
© Joe McIntyre / Simon Middleton

In her biography of her late husband, the widowed Mrs Kingsley explained this apparent scepticism: 'As he often told his own children … he had seen too many ghosts at Barnack to have much respect for them.'

The author Charles Kingsley, who lived at Barnack Rectory in the early 19th century, had much to say about its ghost.

Another famous haunted house in the modern county of Cambridgeshire is Woodcroft Castle, near **Helpston**, formerly in the Soke of Peterborough. This is another medieval house but on a much grander scale than Barnack Rectory, having been converted from a 13th-century castle. Like so many English hauntings, the ghost story of Woodcroft dates from the turbulent days of the Civil War. The manor of Woodcroft was then in the possession of an ardent Royalist, Dr Michael Hudson. Appalled by the predations of Cromwell's New Model Army as they marauded their way through the countryside, without leadership or restraint, Dr Hudson organised a band of militia from the local yeomanry in order to repel them if they strayed too close. Unfortunately, this precaution drew the attention of the Parliamentarian administration and, after a few minor victories, an overwhelming force was sent to crush Hudson's resistance.

Dr Hudson and his band of brothers fell back to Woodcroft Castle but found themselves besieged by the Roundheads. It didn't take too long before the besieging army had broken through their defences and it was even shorter work to dispatch the remaining dispirited yeomen. Dr Hudson, who had fled to the roof, found himself the only survivor. He immediately surrendered but the Roundheads showed no mercy to the man who, as they saw it, had started all the trouble. They forced him over the parapet of the roof. He fell – he clutched the empty air – one hand caught the edge of the roof – and he clung on. But the soldiers were relentless. One of them hacked off his fingers. Dr Hudson plummeted into the moat. Even now, this courageous man was not done for. He managed to swim to the bank, only to be met with equal cruelty. The Roundheads killed him with their pikes. Ever since this dramatic and tragic occurrence, the castle has on occasions resounded to desperate cries of 'Mercy!' and 'Quarter!' and the sounds of fierce fighting.

The echo of a Civil War tragedy is still played out at Woodcroft Castle. The sketch was made by Charles Harper for his book on Haunted Houses published in 1907.

A sad but rather beautiful little story is told of Upwood House at **Upwood**. In 1757 Upwood House was the home of Thomas Hussey, who lived there with his daughter Maria Ann. A wedge had come between father and daughter in the form of Captain Richard Bickerton. Maria Ann was in love with Richard and he with her but a captain's pay was not enough for Mr Hussey, who wanted better for his daughter. He forbade them from marrying. One night, Hussey took a trip to London on business. Maria Ann suddenly woke up to see the curtains round her bed being pulled aside. Her father peered through the gap and smiled down at her before melting back into the darkness. Maria Ann's maid was sleeping in the room and she too saw Thomas Hussey standing by her mistress's bed. The next day the household learnt what the visitation of the previous night had made them fear: that Thomas Hussey was dead. But there was one strand of comfort: Maria Ann was informed that her father's last words were: 'Tell my daughter that I withdraw my opposition to her marriage.' Richard Bickerton proved not only a loving husband but one worthy of Hussey's ultimate trust: in time he became an MP and was made a baronet.

The Old Vicarage at **Grantchester**, just outside Cambridge, became world-famous thanks to war poet Rupert Brooke's poem in commemoration of it. 'The Old Vicarage, Grantchester' was written in 1912 when, perhaps ironically, Brooke was on holiday in Germany, but it became a favourite with First World War soldiers feeling the longing for home shared by soldiers everywhere. Whimsically, Brooke asks:

'yet
Stands the Church clock at ten to three?
And is there honey still for tea?'

The clock on Grantchester's church continued to stand at ten to three for many years, presumably as a tribute to the young poet, who lost his life in Greece during the Great War in 1915. With such a pull towards his home even during his lifetime, perhaps we should not be surprised if his spirit still longs for it. There are claims that Rupert Brooke haunts the Old Vicarage, where he walks about on the top floor and moves books about. Mild poltergeist activity experienced in the summerhouse in the garden has also been put down to Brooke.

If Rupert Brooke does indeed haunt Grantchester, he is not the only literary figure to do so. Lord Byron, another poet who coincidentally also died in Greece but a century earlier, enjoyed summer days in the village during his undergraduate days between 1805 and 1808. The apparition of the young Byron is said to have been glimpsed in and around Grantchester, including at a pool in a nearby nature reserve, where he would enjoy picnics, refreshing himself in the cool, still water. This has been named Byron's Pool in his honour.

George Noel Gordon Lord Byron.

Lord Byron is one of two famous poets said to haunt the environs of Grantchester.
Nicku/Shutterstock

TWO HAUNTED CHURCHES

On May 8, 1885, a gardener returning home from Sawston Hall passed by the Church of St Mary and St John in **Hinxton** and noticed in the graveyard one of his former employers, a Mrs de Freville, standing by the tomb of her husband. The gardener – a Mr Alfred Bard – entered the churchyard with a view to paying his respects to Mrs de Freville. She was dressed in black, with a 'coal-scuttle bonnet' on her head, and she was leaning over the railings, forlornly regarding the memorial. She turned a pale face to Mr Bard but did not acknowledge him. Feeling perhaps a little awkward now, Mr Bard chose not to walk up to Mrs de Freville and passed by five or six yards from her. He stumbled slightly – looked down – looked up again – and was astonished to see that the woman had vanished. And yet there was nowhere for her to vanish to!

Puzzled and a little frightened, Mr Bard noticed that the time on the church clock stood at 9.20pm. When he got home he told his wife about the strange incident. The following day he learnt the news that Mrs de Freville had died the previous day, at 7.30pm – nearly two hours before he saw her apparently alive in Hinxton churchyard. He told the vicar about it and the vicar got in touch with the great paranormal investigator F W H Myers. Myers took written statements from Mr Bard and his wife and wrote about the experience in his important work, *Human Personality and Its Survival After Bodily Death*, published in 1893.

Hinxton churchyard, where a gardener clearly saw his former employer, unaware she had died earlier that day.
© Joe McIntyre / Simon Middleton

St Peter's Church in **Babraham** is also haunted by a phantom woman. In costume of the Victorian period, she has been seen patrolling the graveyard. Whether she is the same as that haunting the interior of the church is uncertain, for this ghost is never seen. Instead, her 'magnificent soprano voice' is heard emanating from one of the stalls. Occasionally a waft of expensive perfume accompanies this rather charming ghost. She can be heard at any time, day or night, but usually on weekdays when the church is empty. Empty, that is, aside from the fortunate witness. However, if the stall she sings from is approached, the singing instantly ceases.

St Peter's Church in Babraham, where ghostly singing has been heard.
© Joe McIntyre / Simon Middleton

Quite unconnected with the ghost of St Peter's are the events of 1466 when a Babraham man named Robert Barker was brought before the Bishop of Ely on the charge of necromancy (i.e. raising up the spirits of the dead). Barker admitted he had acquired from another man a collection of magical kit and caboodle for this purpose, which included: 'A great book; a roll of black art containing characters, circles, exorcisms and conjurations; a hexagonal sheet with strange figures; six metal plates with diverse characters engraved; a chart with hexagonal and pentagonal characters and figures; and gilded wand.' Barker had intended conjuring up spirits so that they could lead him to places where hoards of gold were hidden. He didn't get the chance. He was severely punished and all his conjuring equipment publicly burned in Cambridge.

HAUNTED INNS

Sitting beside the River Ouse in the hamlet of **Holywell**, St Ives, stands the venerable Old Ferry Boat Inn. There is evidence beer has been served on this site since Anglo-Saxon times. The Old Ferry Boat boasts one of England's most celebrated ghosts, that of 'Juliet', who had the courtesy to turn up regular as clockwork on the supposed anniversary of her tragic death, March 17.

Juliet is believed to have lived and died many centuries ago, hers the time-worn tale of a wronged maiden who, abandoned by her lover, gave in to despair and hanged herself. Because she had committed suicide, Juliet's body was debarred from consecrated ground and she was buried under a simple slab of stone beside the river not far from the tree where she chose to end her life. Many years later her gravestone was used to help pave the floor of the Ferry Boat Inn and can still be seen there today. Ever since her resting place was disturbed, Juliet's spirit has visited the Ferry Boat at midnight on March 16/17. It was said her apparition would be seen to rise from the slab and then float through the inn down towards the river. In fact, she has rarely been seen and mysterious noises usually announce her presence.

So regular were Juliet's alleged visits that curious crowds would gather at the inn on the anniversary of her death in the hope of glimpsing her. On one occasion as many as four hundred hopefuls turned up. Antony D Hippisley-Coxe, in his book *Haunted Britain* (Hutchinson 1973), records how 'a boatload of visitors' arrived on the evening of March 16 and asked the landlord when Juliet was likely to appear. 'Tomorrow,' he told them. 'She'll not make herself known tonight.' As he spoke, a tankard hanging from a hook above the bar was sent flying across the room.

Visitors today will find a painted dedication to Juliet on an exposed beam in the ceiling of the public bar. It was added by one of the Old Ferry Boat's previous owners as a tribute to the unhappy maiden whose haunting has brought in so much extra custom over the years.

The Old Ferry Boat Inn at Holywell is one of the most famous haunted pubs in England.
© Joe McIntyre / Simon Middleton

An almost equally well-known haunted hostelry was the Gibbet Inn at **Caxton**. Gibbets were grisly but not uncommon landmarks in earlier centuries. The corpses of criminals were suspended from them in iron cages and they were set up in prominent positions, usually on a roadside, to serve as a deterrent to other would-be felons. A replica of the gibbet at Caxton stands at a roundabout, formerly a crossroads, in place of the original. It is thought the inn may have been built here to take advantage of the crowds who would come to watch each new corpse being hoisted up on display.

It was only a matter of time, though, before one of the innkeepers, one who had a nasty habit of robbing his customers, found his way onto the gibbet himself. One night he crept into a room where three travellers were spending the night, with the intention of stealing the purse from one of them as he slept. Unfortunately, one of the other boarders awoke and saw what was happening. Without thinking, the landlord stabbed the witness and then, in his panic, decided that he had better kill the other two, too, just to make sure. He then dragged the three bodies to a well in the pub and dumped them in it. Such a hasty murder did not go undetected for long and the innkeeper was taken away to be hanged. Soon it was his corpse hanging from the gibbet which had previously done him so much good. There is a ghostly echo of this triple murder in the form of mysterious footsteps which proceed from the door of the room where the boarders were killed and down the staircase, stopping near the foot of the stairs where the old well is located.

The Gibbet Inn became the Caxton Gibbet Hotel in the 1930s but has long since gone. Close to the gibbet, at the time of writing, are the fire-damaged ruins of a Chinese restaurant. It is thought by some that the inn of legend actually stood on this site rather than that of the Caxton Gibbet Hotel. Whichever was the true location, it is unfortunately one which can no longer be visited. However, the gibbet itself, although a replica, possesses an eerie atmosphere, particularly noticeable at twilight when there is little traffic.

The Caxton Gibbet is one of Cambridgeshire's more gruesome landmarks. It stands near the site of an inn where a triple murder took place.
© *Joe McIntyre /Simon Middleton*

Phantom footsteps are also a feature of the Carpenter's Arms in **Great Wilbraham**. They trudge along an upstairs corridor and pause before one of the guest rooms. Then the handle is either rattled by an unseen hand or a knock is heard on the door. Not a few guests over the years have responded to the summons, confused and bleary-eyed, only to find no one on the other side of the door. Unlike the Caxton Gibbet, however, no explanation has been ever been offered for this phenomenon.

Another enigma is the apparition of a 'Quaker' seen in the 1960s in The Bowling Green public house in **Wisbech**. The landlady saw a man dressed in distinctive 18th-century Quaker gear of a long black coat, with a wide-brimmed hat and white neckerchief, coming down the stairs towards her. What made him really spooky was that he was dragging a coffin behind him! Daniel Codd, author of *Mysterious Cambridgeshire*, learnt that in more recent years the pub has also experienced poltergeist activity.

On the High Street in **St Neots**, the New Inn has a ghost dating from the 17th century (rather belying its name). The apparition is said to be that of Henry Rich, First Earl of Holland, who was held prisoner at the inn after the Battle of St Neots. The battle, which took place in 1648, was really more of a skirmish. Rich was in charge of a small band of Royalists who camped overnight in the market square with the intention of marching on to join the forces of King Charles I in the morning. But they were surprised by an army of Roundheads and quickly defeated. Rich's disappointed spirit has haunted the New Inn ever since. A Grey Lady is associated with the Queen's Head in **Harston**. She does not haunt the pub itself but walks past its front door on the way to a little bridge, where she is seen to throw herself into the River Cam running below it.

Another Grey Lady haunts the grand and historic Lion Hotel in **Buckden**. Although many Grey Ladies are the ghosts of nuns, any woman from the past can, of course, have worn a dress in that colour. Evidence this Grey Lady was not a nun is that in life she must have been wearing perfume, for a sweet scent lingers after she has passed by. The even more imposing George Hotel stands opposite the Lion in Buckden. It too is haunted and by none other than legendary highwayman Dick Turpin. Turpin's ghost – and that of his horse Black Bess – is associated with very many old coaching inns up and down the country (another is the White Horse at Eaton Socon). Wearing his trademark tricorn hat, he is said to ride up on Black Bess, who neighs furiously before they both vanish. According to a 1930s travel book, the room where he allegedly stayed was shown to visitors, complete with hidden trapdoor for emergency exits.

In relation to Dick Turpin, this is as good a chapter as any to mention Jeremiah Lagden, a genuine highwayman of the 18th century. He worked as post boy at the White Hart, **Little Abington**, an inn which didn't stay open for long, possibly because it didn't recover its reputation after employing Lagden, who began his criminal career here, stealing from the customers. After becoming a fully-fledged highwayman, robbing coaches on the Newmarket to London road, he set up home in the Old House, Little Abington, where secret compartments in the chimney and under the floor used to be pointed out as places where he hid his booty. Eventually, Lagden was captured and, according to tradition, hanged from a tree in a field opposite the house. His ghost now haunts the village, especially the area near his former home. At one time, parents used the threat of 'Jeremiah' to make sure their kids came in before nightfall.

Two notorious highwaymen are said to haunt Cambridgeshire: Dick Turpin and local lad Jeremiah Lagden.

ANCIENT GHOSTS

Wandlebury Camp is an extensive Iron Age hill fort on top of the Gogmagog Hills, now a country park. The 13th-century writer Gervase of Tilbury relates a story of a 'Martiall spectre or sprite' haunting Wandlebury Camp. According to Gervase: 'If a warrior enters this level space at dead of night, when the moon is shining, and cries '"Knight to knight, come forth!" immediately he will be confronted by a warrior, armed for fight, who, charging horse to horse, either dismounts his adversary or is dismounted.' Gervase describes this as an 'ancient tradition' even in his day.

The legend continues that a Norman knight, Osbert Fitzhugh, decided to have a crack at the spectral knight himself, so one moonlit night he rode out from Cambridge Castle and entered the ramparts of the hill fort, crying: 'Knight to knight, come forth!' Immediately, 'a knight or what looked like a knight' emerged out of the darkness and rode forward to meet him. Osbert and the ghostly knight fought a brutal and hard-fought battle but eventually the living knight proved superior. The ghost knight was unhorsed and sent crashing to the ground. Osbert had been impressed not only by his adversary's prowess but also by the strength and beauty of his horse, a coal-black steed with fiery eyes. He decided to take it with him as his prize. Just as he was leading the horse out of the fort, however, the ghost knight roused himself and hurled a spear, which caught Osbert in his thigh. Then the phantom vanished.

Osbert led the horse to Cambridge Castle, where he tethered it in the courtyard and showed it off as proof of his victory. But he did not enjoy his spoils for long. At daybreak, the animal reared up, pawed the ground and then, snapping its tether like paper, galloped out of the castle courtyard. No one was able to catch it and it was never seen again. Osbert kept one, less welcome, reminder of his clash at Wandlebury Camp, however: every year on the anniversary of the fight the wound where the spear had penetrated his thigh would reopen and bleed anew.

Wandlebury Camp is the setting for one of Cambridgeshire's oldest ghostly legends.
© Joe McIntyre / Simon Middleton

In 1821 another ancient site was discovered at the village of **Litlington**. An area of uncultivated land near the Icknield Way was from time immemorial known by the evocative name of 'Heaven's Walls'. No one really knew why it had this name but one thing the locals were sure of – it was haunted and should be avoided after dark. In 1821 and 1822 excavations here revealed a wall and a number of Roman funerary jars containing ashes of the dead. The land turned out to contain an *ustrinum*, a walled Roman cemetery. 'Heaven's Walls' now seemed an apt name for the place and an explanation for its spooky reputation.

Another intriguing old name is that of Sunken Church Field at **Abington**. Here, states village tradition, there was an ancient church which became a ruin and in time was swallowed up by the ground. It was another place shunned after nightfall, although any alleged haunting seems to have been a benign one. It was said that if on a moonlit night you put your ear to the ground in Sunken Church Field, you might hear the sound of church bells ringing and the eerie singing of a spectral choir. There are a number of other traditions of this sort in the British Isles: in Cumbria, for example, there is a Sunkenkirk with a similar story attached to it, but visible on the ground is a Bronze Age stone circle. Perhaps a similar prehistoric place of worship, rather than a Christian church, is the true origin behind the name at Abington.

Undeniably visible above ground are the Roman remains around the village of **Castor**. Castor comes from the Latin name for a town, *castrum*. The remains of a Roman settlement, which stood alongside Ermine Street, are visible as humps and lumps in the fields and many artefacts from this period have been found by locals as well as archaeologists. One of these is a raised track, possibly a buried wall, which runs north from the river. The locals called it 'my Lady Conyburrow's Way'. A coney is a country name for a rabbit, and 'coney burrow' is clearly a clumsy version of the name of Castor church's patron saint, St Kyneburgha, or as scholars prefer to spell it, St Cyneburg. St Cyneburg was a 7th-century princess, one of the daughters of Penda, King of Mercia. Castor is the only church in Britain dedicated to her. Although she was married to a prince of Northumbria, St Cyneburg later became a Benedictine nun and founded a convent at Castor with her sister St Cyneswith.

The legend given to explain the origin of Lady Conyburrow's Way is that although St Cyneburg had taken a vow of chastity, a local 'ruffian' attempted to have his way with her. In order to preserve her honour, the pure-hearted maiden ran through the fields along where the track can now be seen. One version of the tale states that the track miraculously raised itself out of the ground to aid her flight, her pursuer becoming entangled in the undergrowth; another that the path only became apparent subsequent to the adventure as a memorial to her 'purity and innocence'.

The early antiquarian William Stukeley, writing in the 18th century, recorded a further tradition, one of a ghostly nature. He was told by the villagers that St Cyneburg reappeared in Castor 'some few nights before Michaelmas' and rode through the fields in a phantom coach. Although he describes her route as along a Roman road through the fields, it is probably Lady Conyburrow's Way he is referring to. Stukeley believed the tale might have been a vague memory of an Anglo-Saxon festival in which the saint's relics would have been carried in a procession on the anniversary of her death, September 15.

The ancient village of Castor has a ghost which dates back to the Dark Ages.

An amusing ghost story attached to a prehistoric monument comes from **Whittlesford**. Before they were flattened by the local squire in the early 19th century, there were three burial mounds near Whittlesford which went by the evocative name of the Chronicle Hills (also known, more prosaically, as the Conical Hills). During their levelling, Roman remains, including two skeletons, were unearthed.

The skeletons were found in a most unusual position: locked together as if fighting a furious battle in the grave. One of the labourers employed by the squire to level the mounds decided to take home a souvenir: one of the two skulls. He placed it in a prominent place on his bedroom mantelpiece.

Mr Matthews – that was the name of the labourer – didn't get much sleep, though. As soon as he'd put his head down there came an insistent knocking at his front door. Annoyed at having his rest disturbed, Matthews stuck his head out of the bedroom window, intending to tell whoever it was to clear off. Imagine his shock when he saw, standing in the garden, a headless skeleton, shaking its bony fist at him. Despite now lacking of a mouth of any description, the skeleton, 'in a hoarse, sepulchral voice', demanded the restitution of his headbone. The foolish Matthews cried out in terror and dived back under the bedclothes. On the following night he received another visit from the skeleton, which again demanded the return of its skull. This went on for a few more nights until Matthews finally had the sense to open the window and throw the skull down to its rightful owner. The skeleton scooped it up, returned from whence it came and Matthews' rest was not disturbed again.

HOUNDS OF HELL

There are many accounts of huge and hellish hounds haunting the British countryside. Usually they are described as black in colour and of enormous size, far bigger than any breed of dog today. Sometimes they have a shaggy coat, often fiery red eyes, or even just one eye glowing fiercely in the middle of their foreheads. Occasionally they are headless. In most parts of the country they are eerily silent, with the nasty habit of creeping up on night-bound travellers and literally dogging their footsteps down darkened lanes. However, in East Anglia in particular, they can be very noisy, setting up a frightful howl after dark. In this part of the country, too, they are considered evil omens: to see or hear one may be a warning of impending illness or death. These supernatural Black Dogs go by a number of regional names, such as Skriker and Padfoot; in Cambridgeshire they are known as Shucky or Black Shuck.

J Wentworth Day, a country squire and author who spent his happiest hours among the fens and waterways of the eastern low counties, collected many stories about Black Shuck. Half a century or so ago, after an evening spent duck hunting in the then much wilder and more extensive **Wicken Fen**, Day asked if anyone in the local pub would like to accompany him back home. His route was along an ancient causeway that had been raised in Saxon times to allow safe passage through the marshes. The tough old countrymen present that night all politely declined, one telling him (in the local dialect): 'That owd Black Dog run there o' nights, master. Do ye goo, he'll have ye as sure as harvest.'

Another man, an old fellow called Fred, who had taught Wentworth Day many of his skills with line and gun, also refused the offer, saying that his own sister had seen the 'owd Dog' as she was on her way to meet her sweetheart at a moonlit tryst.

'Big as a calf, sir, he come along that bank quiet as death,' said Fred. 'Jest padded along head down, gret old ears flappin'. That worn't more'n twenty yards off when that raised that's head and glouted [glared] at her – eyes red as blood. My heart! She did holler. She let out a shrik like an owd owl and belted along that there back like a hare. Run sir! There worn't nuthin' could ha' ketched her. She come bustin' along that bank like a racehoss, right slap into her young man. Ha! She did holler. And then, when he collared hold of her, she went off dead in a faint!'

A supernatural Black Dog is said to patrol Wicken Fen.
Radek Sturgolewski/Shutterstock

Another author, Rupert Matthews, lists several other locations in Cambridgeshire where Black Shuck has been seen: the villages of **West Wickham**, **West Wratting** and **Balsham**, and the ancient earthwork known as the Devil's Ditch at **Reach**. Joan Forman, in her *Haunted East Anglia*, records a sighting in Cambridge itself. She writes: 'One evening Mrs Duval and her husband were driving along Arbury Road [in the northern suburbs]. The time of year was midsummer, and darkness still lay an hour or two ahead. It was apparently a pleasant evening and neither occupant of the car was prepared for what happened. Without warning, a huge, black wolf-like animal appeared and leapt over the bonnet of the car. The Duvals' car was of the vintage type with a long bonnet, and the leap across it needed considerable power and agility. The animal vanished into an allotment on the far side of the road, and although the couple at once left their car and searched the area no trace of the creature was found. What the Duvals did notice, however, was a sensation of extreme cold, in spite of the summer weather and the abject terror of their own dog, which they had left in the back of the car.'

Just as the legends state, the sighting of this Black Dog proved a harbinger of misfortune: the couple suffered a devastating financial loss shortly afterwards and the husband was diagnosed with a condition that proved to be fatal. Forman points out that Arbury is the site of an Iron Age Settlement and, like so many other writers, notes the great antiquity of these strange and fearsome phantoms, and ponders whether they represent the folk memories of wolves or other prehistoric animals. The Arbury Road phantom is described as 'wolf-like'. Just over the Cambridgeshire border into Norfolk, at **Southery**, there is a tale of a huge, feral wolf/wolfhound hybrid that was killed after it attacked monks seeking to found a church there in the early Middle Ages. The ghost of this animal is supposed to still haunt the area, howling horribly on the anniversary of its death – and the founding of the church – May 29.

Generally, however, the Black Dogs are described as resembling hounds of the mastiff breed, much shorter in body and snout than a wolf. Their much greater size and other paranormal characteristics suggest they are not simply the ghosts of ordinary animals that have passed on but something much stranger. In Cambridgeshire, however, there is a rare example of a story told to explain one of these spooks in terms of a ghostly pet. Like so many tales from the county, it was collected by folklorist Enid Porter. The setting is the minor road which runs parallel to the A10, on the other side of the Great Ouse river. On this road, half way between **Littleport** and **Brandon Creek**, a fatal accident occurred one foggy night when a panicky horse plunged into the river, taking its rider with it. The dead man's dog remained at the scene of the tragedy, patrolling the lane and the river bank, howling out its grief. It continued to do so as a ghost, its unearthly howls keeping the local residents awake. It would follow travellers down the road, some of whom reported feeling its 'hot breath against their legs'.

This version of Black Shuck no longer haunts the road, however. In 1906, a man driving home in an early motorcar collided with something big and black in the fog just at the spot where the original accident occurred. He got out but could find nothing in the road to account for his collision. And that was the end of the haunting. The spectral dog's howls were never heard again and no more did pedestrians need to fear being followed by him down the lane. This must be the only example on record of Black Shuck being run over!

The mysterious Black Dogs of British folklore, such as Cambridgeshire's Black Shuck, are usually described as being huge examples of the mastif breed

Other **GHOST STORIES** for you to enjoy from
BRADWELL BOOKS

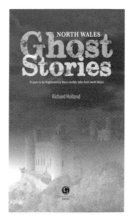

More **GHOST STORIES** from
BRADWELL BOOKS on next page

More **GHOST STORIES** from
BRADWELL BOOKS on next page

BRADWELL
BOOKS